Angel-grams

Messages and Miracles by Special Delivery

by
Heather Down

Cover Illustration by MarketForce
Typography by MarketForce, Burr Ridge, IL

Published by Great Quotations Publishing Co.,
Glendale Heights, IL

Library of Congress Catalog Number: 98-75440

ISBN: 1-56245-357-2

Printed in Hong Kong

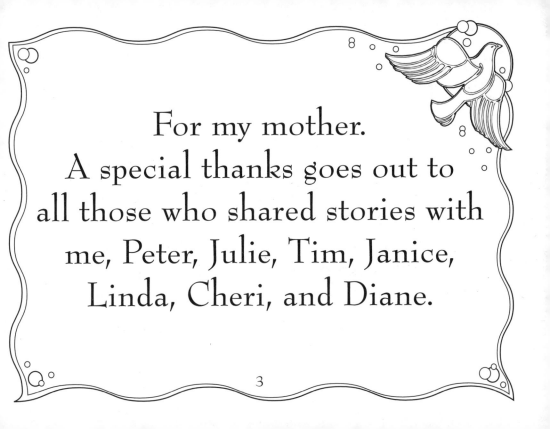

For my mother.
A special thanks goes out to
all those who shared stories with
me, Peter, Julie, Tim, Janice,
Linda, Cheri, and Diane.

Forward

Coincidence, fate, miracles, or luck. Whatever you choose to name it, destined occurrences happen over and over. It may not be confirmed by science, yet it is affirmed by hearts everywhere. Our lives move with a rhythm and pattern too precise to be haphazard. It is those everyday, little things, that constantly remind us that Someone is watching over and caring for us.

This collection of thoughts and stories is based on just one person's circle of knowledge and friends. You would be hard pressed to find anyone alive who had never experienced a defining moment. Near misses or little insights, these moments shape us, mold us, and remind us that there are days when we indeed receive aid by special delivery.

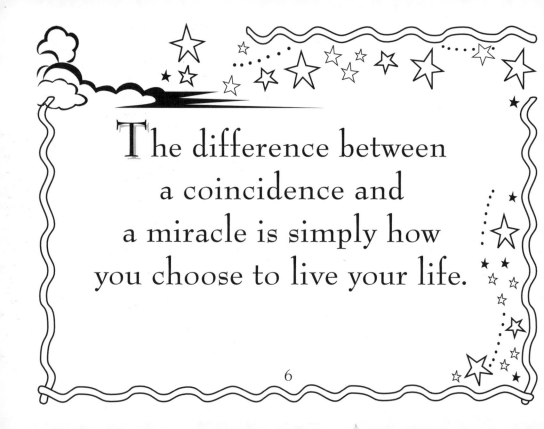

The difference between
a coincidence and
a miracle is simply how
you choose to live your life.

Some days you know your guardian angels are working. Other days you may not be aware of them. But, you can be assured they are working just as hard during those times.

7

If guardian angels get paid double for overtime, mine ought to be a multi-billionaire by now!

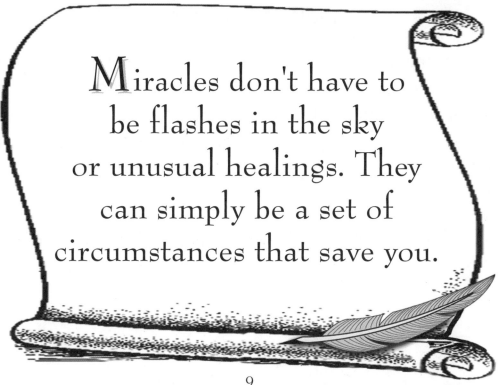

Miracles don't have to
be flashes in the sky
or unusual healings. They
can simply be a set of
circumstances that save you.

Angels in My Pocket

Seventeen year old John Denny unpacked his bags in the third class room on the ship docked in Liverpool. He was excited about setting across the great Atlantic to start a new life at a fruit orchard in Canada. An hour and a half before departure he received a wireless. His only aunt had suffered a stroke!

The event and timing seemed so unfortunate. He repeated the words over in his head "Death imminent, please come home to family."

Little did he know how very true that statement was.

He loved his family and he knew he must leave the ship. Repacking his belongings and moving out of steerage, he traveled to be back with his elderly, sick aunt. Sometime later, John would reach into one of his coat pockets and find a ticket stub for the Titanic, and in the other, a pocket full of angels.

Think of all the near misses when you know your guardian angel was close by. Now, imagine the many more times you don't know about!

Praise ye him, all his angels:
praise ye him, all his hosts.

Psalms 148:2 KJV

Someday, it would be nice to thank the angels face to face.

14

Fall of Grace

For this retired high school teacher, building his own cottage was a dream come true. He placed his step ladder near the opening for the yet unfinished stairwell which was currently covered with a layer of blue styrofoam. Suddenly, all went black.

A strange, loud, agonizing sound filled his ears. It was like a wild animal enraged, roaring in the background. Time passed in slow motion until the man had a startling revelation. Every time he took a breath, the noise stopped. He realized that the noise was, in fact, coming from him.

He concluded that he had fallen off his ladder and through the opening for the stair well. His body had careened two stories onto the solid concrete floor where he lay flat on his back in unbelievable pain.

Rolling over, he examined the blue foam that he had taken down squarely underneath him. He shuddered uncontrollably as he looked at the spots that had become pancake thin as a result of the impact. A little shift one way or another would have been fatal. Although he sustained two compression fractures in his back, time and grace healed him fully. He has no recollection of the fall, but the impact of it remains in his life constantly.

Guardian angels watch over you.
Mine also regularly checks
underneath me, and to either
side, especially at intersections!

Angels work hard to keep you safe, sane, and saved.

The work of an angel
is never done.

Angels don't have to take human form. Just ask the owner of a seeing eye dog.

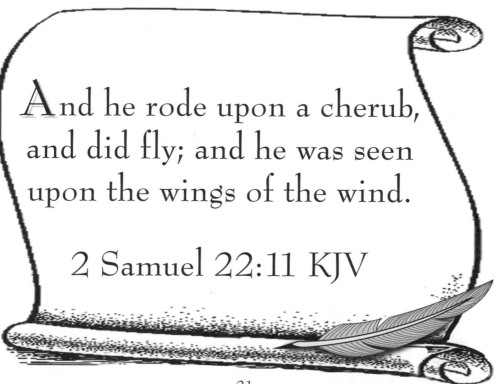

And he rode upon a cherub, and did fly; and he was seen upon the wings of the wind.

2 Samuel 22:11 KJV

Flying with the Angels

Nine year old Kristin had no idea what the day would bring as she flew down a steep hill on her bicycle in Aalesund, Norway. Her thoughts were elsewhere when she missed the stop sign and found herself in the middle of an intersection. Neither driver nor cyclist had time to react as the oncoming car hit the girl and sent her flying into the air.

Stunned and panicked, the driver stopped to help the stricken girl. The driver of a nearby cargo truck filled with panes of glass also stopped to help the injured cyclist. Shocked and confused, both drivers could not find the girl anywhere.

The bicycle was accounted for but no girl could be found. They looked under the vehicles, in the ditches, and in nearby grass, but found nothing.

The driver who hit Kristin started questioning his sanity. Was this just a bad dream? It couldn't be for the truck driver had witnessed the accident also. Taking one last desperate look around, the man finally spotted Kristin. There, sitting in between the realms of glass, sat the dazed girl.

Kristin sustained bumps and bruises, but had no serious injuries. An angel must have brought her down in the cargo bed of the glass company truck, somehow missing the panes of glass stacked in upright racks.

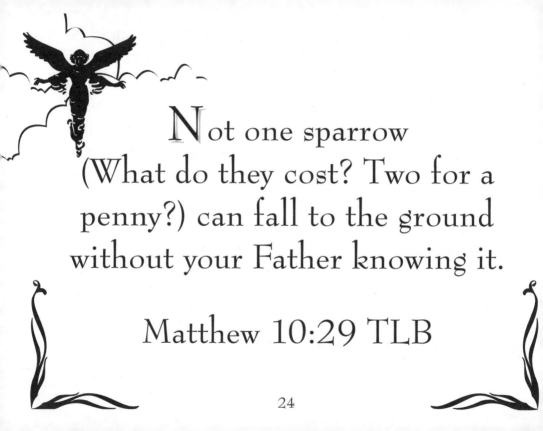

Not one sparrow (What do they cost? Two for a penny?) can fall to the ground without your Father knowing it.

Matthew 10:29 TLB

Kelly

Kelly was a runaway Shetland Sheepdog, destined for the pound. Her lovable disposition and affectionate ways soon found her a home, however. She tormented the children's stuffed animals, unconditionally loved her owners, romped with the owner's older dog, and came in first in her class in obedience and agility. Then, one day, seven months after she had been placed there, she dropped dead, probably due to an aneurism, at a year and a half of age.

8   The family mourned and buried her in the backyard. They did not understand why this had happened. In speaking to a friend about this misfortune, she told the family, "True, you didn't have Kelly very long, but an angel must have been looking out for her. I know you only had her for 7 months, but those were probably the best 7 months of her life. She was lucky to have had you."

An angel doesn't have to have wings and a halo. An angel can take on a variety of forms: it can be a smiling child, a stranger who gives directions, or a gas attendant.

You don't have to go to the gates of heaven to see an angel, just open your eyes and look around.

H ope lives in belief.

Be not forgetful to
entertain strangers:
for thereby some have
entertained angels unawares.

Hebrews 13:2 KJV

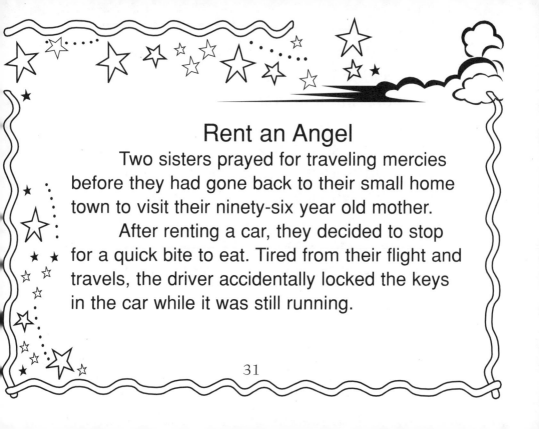

Rent an Angel

Two sisters prayed for traveling mercies before they had gone back to their small home town to visit their ninety-six year old mother.

After renting a car, they decided to stop for a quick bite to eat. Tired from their flight and travels, the driver accidentally locked the keys in the car while it was still running.

Worried and frustrated, the women decided to call the rental company from a pay phone in the fast food restaurant. Pulling out her rental contract, the driver dialed the number. It was later in the evening on a weekend and the office was closed. Would there be anyone in this small town who could help them now?

A man sitting close by happened to notice their contract. He recognized the company logo on the paper. "Do you have a problem?" he inquired.

The women explained their plight and the kind stranger smiled. His neighbor worked for that particular rental company. He could give him a call.

The man called his neighbor and explained the situation. Within 20 minutes the company employee drove to the closed office, opened it up, picked up a spare key, and delivered it to the restaurant. Unbelievably grateful, the women did not cause their mother any worry as they arrived on schedule!

Sometimes angels can work through some very ungodly vessels.

If you haven't seen a miracle today, create one.

It is possible for humans to display angelic qualities. Nelson Mandela, Mohandas Gandhi, and Mother Teresa have proved it to be so.

Behold, I send an Angel before thee, to keep thee in the way, and to bring thee into the place which I have prepared.

Exodus 23:20 KJV

Angel in Overalls

The heat gauge on the car was reading dangerously high and the young woman traveling alone didn't want to blow the engine. Without a cell phone she felt nervous. She pulled into the nearest highway service center and whispered a prayer. She checked the oil level and it was fine but she wondered about the radiator. Putting her hand on the cap, she realized that it was much too hot to open. It was necessary to stay put until it cooled.

Although he was a couple of hundred miles away, she phoned her father. He was concerned and wanted to see her home, safe and sound.

The engine had time to cool so she drove over to the service attendant. She told him her story of the elevated heat gage. He opened the radiator cap and checked the water level and topped off the depleted supply off. She was grateful and asked him how much she owed him.

"Nothing," he quickly responded.

She thanked him emphatically and as she thought about her recent conversation with her father, she added, "And my father thanks you too."

He seemed reflective for a moment. He then topped off the coolant and gave the woman the excess fluid left in the bottle to keep in the car. Although worth several dollars he told her not to worry about it and just have a safe trip home to her father. As she drove off she realized she hadn't even bothered to purchase any gas there.

I don't think angels work
in time and space as we know it.
I don't think they communicate
with words, letters or language as
we do. I think they work on the
principle of 'a twinkling of an eye.'

In a moment, in the twinkling of an eye, at the last trump: for the trumpet shall sound, and the dead shall be raised incorruptible, and we shall be changed.

1 Corinthians 15:52 KJV

Like the angels,
we don't need to depend
solely on our ears to listen.
We can learn just as much
in silence as in noise.

A mother's love is angelic.

Angel-gram

My mother is an incredible person. When I was young, I was sure that she used a ruler when she made beds - just to make sure that the blankets hung exactly even on both sides. This science of precision bed-making would put most hospitals and army camps to shame.

Another endearing quality of my mother was the fact that she always slept with both ears open. Even through closed bedroom doors she would always hear my barely audible scared whispers through the deep, dark of night, "Mom....Mom.... Mom-my."

Whether a bad dream, a night monster, or a wet bed, my mother always sprang into immediate consciousness and came to my complete and utter rescue while the rest of the household slept peacefully.

Life moved on and I moved out. With a long time and distance between us, I carved out an existence and family of my own. But, she continues to hear my silent calls, and somehow knows when to telephone when I need her most.

"Mom...Mom...Mom-my."

No matter how old I am, my mother will always listen in her sleep, only now, instead of her ears, it is her heart that she keeps open to the whispers of angels.

I wonder if we are ever angels in the eyes of others?

Ask not what the angels can do for you, but what you can do for the angels.

Sometimes angels whisper softly in your ear, other times it may be necessary for them to scream at the top of their lungs.

If angels were to keep
a list of all your
acts of kindness,
how fast would they
run out of ink?

Caught in the Headlights

Stepping out of my car in a busy department store parking lot, I noticed that the headlights on the car next to mine were left on. There was no one in the car and I knew that the lights would wear on the battery. Instead of taking down the license number and getting the store to page the owner, I pushed away a twinge of guilt by rationalizing that I was in a hurry. It really wasn't my problem anyway. Quickly, I hustled by the car and into the store.

Roaming up and down busy aisles with a cart, I completed my shopping errands. As I stood in the check out line an hour later, I felt relieved to have finished my trek. I grabbed the packaged bags of new belongings and headed for my car. Shame and astonishment swept over me as I looked at my car. There, shining into my face, were my own dimming headlights.

Dropping my head, I realized how selfish I had been. I had an opportunity to be someone's angel, but instead I denied myself the privilege and it truly was my loss.

When are we
too old to believe in angels?
Never.

Know ye not that they which
run in a race run all,
but one receiveth the prize?
Do run, that ye may obtain.

1 Corinthians 9:24 KJV

An angel without action would be like spaghetti without the sauce - incomplete and tasteless.

What would happen
if we all had the
confidence of angels?

Angelic Confidence

Walking through a local flea market, my daughter was enticed by a man who was conducting frog races. Seeing her interest, he was hoping that he could coax her into betting on a frog.

"Come on, young lady, race a frog," he advertised.

She looked at him in disbelief and answered his pleading in all sincerity, "Ah, come on. You're crazy. I could beat a frog any day!"

I reflected for a moment. How very powerful we would be if we all possessed the confidence of angels that she had.

Have faith.

There are dozens of promises
just waiting to be claimed.
Don't hesitate to get in line.

If you want to receive,
you have to ask!

Ask, and it shall be given you; seek, and ye shall find; knock, and it shall be opened unto you.

Matthew 7:7 KJV

Be Careful What You Ask For!

A small group of young adults were camping in very late fall. It was extremely cold and had rained for two days straight. Crawling into a rather uninviting, damp, frigid, sleeping bag, one woman prayed, "Lord, please make it stop raining tomorrow."

The next morning the young lady awoke to find her prayers had been answered. She wished that she had been more specific, however. It was no longer raining - it was snowing!

62

Some people don't believe
in angels, but remember,
some people used to believe
the world was flat!

Live on the edge,
believe in miracles

Cast thy burden upon the
Lord, and he shall sustain thee:
he shall never suffer the
righteous to be moved.

Psalms 55:22 KJV

I'm sure that the angels carry us when we have no strength left to carry ourselves.

Say Good-Bye

A young woman was rushed in an ambulance into the emergency room. A very bad car accident had injured her. Conscious and very coherent, she phoned her parents to tell them of her unfortunate circumstances. Swiftly, the worried mother and father rushed to the hospital. They spoke, laughed, and reaffirmed their love for each other when she drifted into unconsciousness and then unexpected death.

Wondering why someone who entered the hospital so healthy was so quickly lost, an independent inquiry was set up. There was concern that maybe a rib had been broken in the hospital and may have punctured a lung. The investigation was very conclusive. There was no explanation as to how the young woman had survived the accident at all. Scientifically, she should have been dead at the scene. Her sustained life and good bye to her parents were nothing short of a miracle.

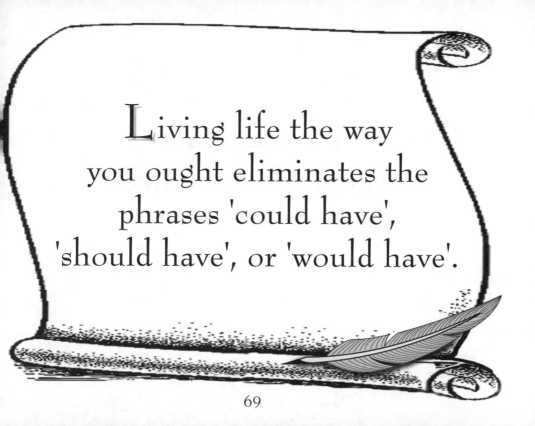

Living life the way
you ought eliminates the
phrases 'could have',
'should have', or 'would have'.

Miracles are
everyday occurrences.

God reveals Himself
in unique ways.

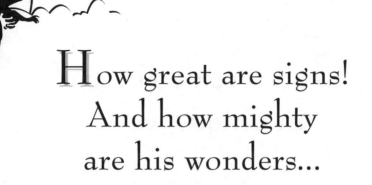

How great are signs!
And how mighty
are his wonders...

Daniel 4:3 KJV

Angels Dancing in the Sky

The woman had never seen the Aurora Borealis before. That night the northern lights flickered and played in the sky like dancing rainbows. To her, they seemed liked a promise, lights of hope, a sign that everything would be okay.

The woman had just lost her father and she was spending the night at the old farm house with her mother. While watching the brilliant display in the sky, the phone rang. It was the woman's brother telling her to look towards the east. She ran to the other side of the house to see the lights moving in a different manner, forming a picture almost that of an angel.

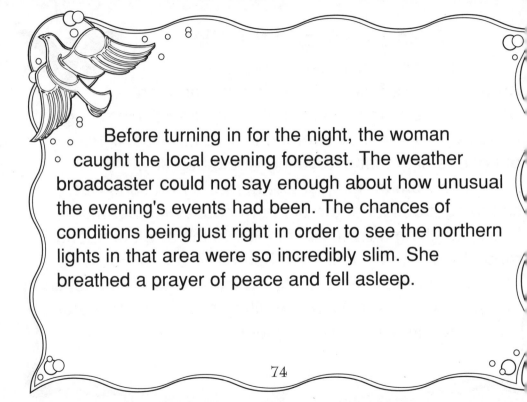

Before turning in for the night, the woman caught the local evening forecast. The weather broadcaster could not say enough about how unusual the evening's events had been. The chances of conditions being just right in order to see the northern lights in that area were so incredibly slim. She breathed a prayer of peace and fell asleep.

Angels mean messengers
and ministers. Their function
is to execute the plan of divine
providence, even in earthly things.

Saint Thomas Aquinas

One angelic act can hide
a hundred mortal flaws.

Faith can give you peace
that money cannot buy.

The most valuable gifts
have no price tag:
faith, hope, love, and time.

And now abideth faith, hope, charity, these three; but the greatest of these is charity.

1 Corinthians 13:13 KJV

Angels in the Septic Bed

At the time, this twenty-six year old teacher had no idea how important her decision to trade yard supervision duty times was. While out watching the children, a young boy of nine ran through the out-of-bounds area in front of the school. The grass was currently being dug up as the septic bed was being replaced. The teacher ran after the boy, yelling at him to come back but he dodged around the mounds of earth and completely out of sight.

Furious at his disobedience, the teacher went to the vice-principal to report the antics of this student, demanding that the student be called into the office at once.

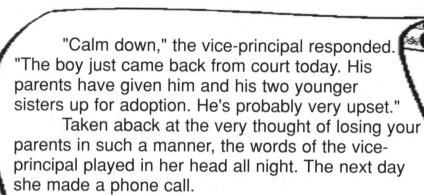

"Calm down," the vice-principal responded. "The boy just came back from court today. His parents have given him and his two younger sisters up for adoption. He's probably very upset."

Taken aback at the very thought of losing your parents in such a manner, the words of the vice-principal played in her head all night. The next day she made a phone call.

Four months later, the boy and his two sisters were legally adopted by the teacher and her husband. Besides the boy, there must have been a few angels running through the septic bed that day also!

You find what you are looking for. If you seek evil, you will see it, if you seek good, you will become it.

An angel is anyone who saves
another from destruction.

If I speak in the tongues of men and of angels, but have not love, I am only a resounding gong or a clanging cymbal...

1 Corinthians 13:1-3

My guardian angel
works in one gear – high.

Angels direct and guide us.

Guiding Angel

He had broken his ankle in a sky diving accident, of all things. The young wife had received the phone call and started up the car. She was half way to the sky diving school when she realized she had no idea where the town where her husband lay in a hospital bed was. She rifled through the glove compartment and found no maps, not even old ones. Frustrated she drove forward. He needed surgery.

She took a deep breath and kept on driving. As if on automatic pilot, the woman drove right to the town, and then straight to the hospital. After visiting with her husband, she began to think about the remarkable feat of arriving without directions. She asked a nearby nurse what the most direct route from the hospital to her town was. Not terribly surprising, but she had taken the most direct route possible.

The smallest angelic act can make the biggest difference.

Some angels don't have
wings and a halo but
work boots and dirty hands.

What is an Angel?

To the woman just out of the hospital, it was the lady who offered to clean up the spilled milk in the fridge. To the young mother, it was the man who spotted her boy chase his stray ball out into the street. To the teacher, it was the student who said thank you.

Just because it can be explained, doesn't make it any less a miracle. Modern medicine isn't any less a miracle to those it saves.

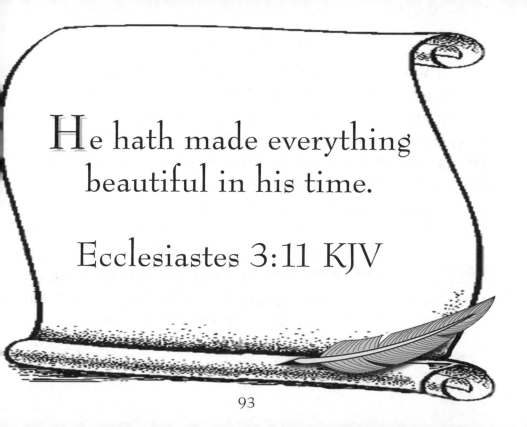

He hath made everything beautiful in his time.

Ecclesiastes 3:11 KJV

In His Time

The eleven year old girl woke up complaining about severe abdominal pains. The mother called the doctor to find out when the next available opening for an appointment would be. He could see her at 4:00 p.m. but felt that the little girl should go to the hospital. The mother protested, saying it was probably just the flu. But, the doctor did not relent. "Take her to the hospital."

The young girl complained. She did not want to go to the hospital. Couldn't she wait until 4:00 p.m. and visit the doctor in his office? Against her better judgement, the mother took her daughter to the hospital anyway.

Within a couple of hours it was determined that the girl had acute appendicitis. She was prepped for surgery and her own doctor was called in to assist. He came and prayed with the girl before the operation. As the incision was made, the appendix completely ruptured. This potentially life threatening occurrence happened at 4:00 p.m., the earliest time she could have seen her doctor. Angels had kept watchful time that day.

Show me an act of mercy
and I'll show you an angel.

Should angels apply for
any other job,
they would be over qualified.

Our halos may be broken
and our wings a little crooked,
but we all have potential.

In all their affliction
he was afflicted, and the
angel of his presence saved
them: in his love and in his pity he
redeemed them; and he bare them,
and carried them all the days of old.

Isaiah 63:9 KJV

Angel Right on Track

The engineer spotted the object on the tracks. It looked like a small animal, or a pile of wood but as the train drew closer he realized that it was a small child. The brakes were immediately pulled, and the whistle blown, but the object did not move. The situation looked desperate. There simply was no chance of stopping in time, so the man crawled out to the front of the train.

Knowing that this was his only chance, he leaned forward and pressed his leg as far out in front as he could. At just the right moment, he kicked the child off the track in time to save the boy from being run over. His angelic act worked, and the young child survived with a only a broken arm.

Have you ever seen an angel?
If you have seen a newborn
baby, a child laugh, or a proud
parent, you have seen an angel!

Guardian angels don't have time to take coffee breaks.

...And, behold, angels came and ministered unto him.

Matthew 4:11 KJV

Human kindness is a miracle.

Miracle in a Paint Tin

Her bottom lip was quivering uncontrollably and her eyes were welling up. For this little four year old junior kindergarten girl, painting seemed like a very scary task. It was new, brand new to her and very, very, daunting. The teacher noticed the little girl's apprehension and put her arm around her. Gently, she guided the girl's hand around the brush, into the paint tin, and

onto the paper. The girl's lip stopped quivering, and soon she was almost giggling. In a very short time she required no more assistance and was painting greens, reds, blues, and yellows, wildly all over her paper. The girl went home with the miracle of discovery and the teacher went home with the miracle of re-discovery.

My children are angels.......
when they are sleeping.

108

For if the word spoken by angels was steadfast, and every transgression and disobedience received a just recompense of reward;

Hebrews 2:2 KJV

The Clandestine Hair Cut

A rebellious young boy did not want to get a haircut. In protest to his mother's request, he climbed a nearby pole. Although it was easy going up, he was unable to get down. Emergency services were called. Before they could reach him, however, he fell and was rushed to the hospital. Although he was not seriously hurt, the doctor needed to shave the boy's head in order to treat the injuries. The boy who didn't want a hair cut got more than he bargained for. After the incident he didn't need a hair cut for a very long time.

Angels don't hide in churches.
They work in homes,
hearts, and dark alleys.

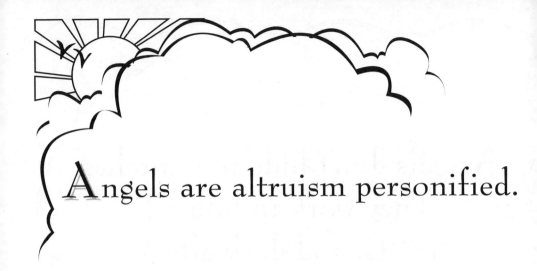

Angels are altruism personified.

Angels have an incredible
sense of timing.

Angels guard without bars,
keys or locks, but with love,
protection and concern.

114

He is the Angel who has kept me from all harm....

Genesis 48:16 KJV

Central Heaven Time

The country road was dark and deserted. Why did her car have to break down here? The only thing close by was an unlit farm house. A pick-up truck drove slowly by with a lone sinister looking driver who stared intently at the stranded woman. A moment ticked by when she realized the truck had turned around and was headed back her way.

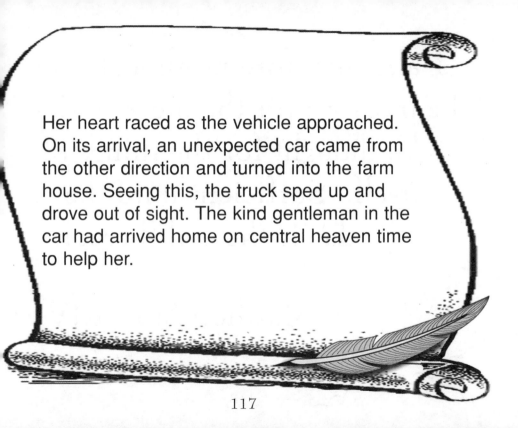

Her heart raced as the vehicle approached. On its arrival, an unexpected car came from the other direction and turned into the farm house. Seeing this, the truck sped up and drove out of sight. The kind gentleman in the car had arrived home on central heaven time to help her.

Take therefore no thought for the morrow; for the morrow shall take thought for the things of itself. Sufficient unto the day is the evil thereof.

Matthew 6:34 KJV

...Your Father knoweth what things ye have need of, before ye ask him.

Matthew 6:8 KJV

The best dividends
aren't paid in money.

Invest in your angel.
Put stock in God
and buy into prayer.

Mutual Funds

There was no doubt, he needed money for groceries. Things were very tight for him and his family. Getting ready to go out, he put on his sports jacket. As he slipped his keys into his pocket he felt some bills. He pulled out ten twenty dollar bills and an ATM slip dated six months ago. He smiled to himself. He and his angels had set up a little mutual fund for this occasion.

Angels may sit on clouds,
but they walk on earth.

If belief in angels
is a drug for the masses,
then it is the healthiest
legalized pharmaceutical around!

The Lottery

Due to downsizing, someone had to be transferred out to another location. There were several employees with equal seniority so a lottery was held. A young woman received the losing ticket. For a variety of reasons, this move was more than inconvenient, it was devastating. Others avoided eye contact in the hallways and very few spoke to her about her unexpected move - except Margaret.

She left a poem on a note in her mailbox:

We know you must be feeling bad,
But we think you are a star.
We hope that things will work out
So you stay right where you are
    (With us!)
    Margaret

The woman thanked Margaret and Margaret responded, "I felt so bad when I heard. It could have just as easily been me."

Due to several retirements, the woman was able to happily transfer back. Margaret started to complain of abdominal pain. Seven months later this mother of two had passed away with pancreatic cancer.

The woman has placed her note by the light switch in her bedroom. It is the last thing she sees before falling asleep at night as it reminds her of how precious the gift of life is. Margaret's words still ring in her ears, "It could have just as easily been me."

If given the opportunity,
side with the angels.

Do enough
to keep your angels
employed.

He delivers his people, preserving them from harm; he does great miracles in heaven and earth; it is he who delivered Daniel from the power of the lions.

Daniel 6:27 TLB

Angel at the Well

A five year old and his brother were bundled up and sent out to play on a wintry day. Little Tim's long, woolen scarf was tied snugly around his neck. An old, motorized well pump sprung into action and intrigued the young boy. As he got close, the fringes of his scarf caught in the rickety moving parts. Terrified, he felt his scarf tighten around his neck. The boy pulled back with all his might. His brother stood watching, frozen in horror. The machine continued to eat the scarf, pulling the little boy closer to certain destruction. Tim put his hands on his knees, elbows locked in attempt to resist against the force.

"Dear God," was all he could say.

At that moment, a clear hand seemed to swiftly swipe through the woolen scarf and Tim fell backwards. Grabbing the two pieces of the scarf, the boys ran into the safety of the house. Tim's mother placed the two halves of the scarf on the table to view the cleanest, straightest edge she had ever witnessed.

Every once in a while
someone will touch your life
and you will no longer be the
same. You must have been
touched by an angel.

And to you who are troubled, rest with us, when the Lord Jesus shall be revealed from heaven with his mighty angels.

2 Thessalonians 1:7

Just a Note

No one could read her mind. On the outside all was well. She had a nice home, lovely job, beautiful family, yet inside she was weeping. She felt worthless, small, and unappreciated. No one knew she was questioning her very existence.

Then, she noticed an envelope on her desk. She read the note, "I felt impressed to leave you this note. I really admire you and think you are a wonderful person. I wish I could give you more; I realize that it is just a note."

Just a note that had made all the difference in one woman's life.

Don't look at the rain if you can catch a glimpse of the sun. Don't look at the million things to do, if you can see what's done. Don't watch a sunset if you can see it rise. A positive outlook will make you healthier, happier, and wise.

A merry heart maketh a cheerful countenance: but by sorrow of the heart the spirit is broken.

Proverbs 15:30 KJV

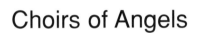

Choirs of Angels

Along with tulips, a myriad of forgotten treasures sprouted on our lawn with the final melting of the winter snow. The dog's towel, a utility ball, a hockey net, three bicycles, a really good pair of winter gloves, well used plastic containers, a screw driver, and many other novelty items decorated both the front and back yard. Since the majority of these geological finds belonged to my two pre-teen daughters, they were encouraged, then later commissioned, to clean up the yard. Discord over duty, equity, fairness and sibling rivalry surfaced uglier than the messy lawn itself.

I prayed for help and help arrived. Upon putting the hockey nets away, one daughter discovered an old radio in the garage. She plugged it in and upbeat music wafted into the back yard. Suddenly, the bickering turning into singing and the entire tone changed. It truly was heavenly music.

Remember to count your blessings. It makes you a happier person.

Wouldn't it be nice to have the perspective of angels?

Perspective

It's funny how we can withstand life-changing pressures but buckle under the stress of gooey globs of toothpaste stuck to the sides of the sink, flat tires, stubbed toes, undelivered phone messages, drivers who don't signal, ketchup stains on silk, misplaced scissors, keys inside locked cars, inoperable ball point pens, and empty toilet paper rolls. It takes angelic patience to deal with life's little trials.

We humans marvel in our technology. Think about how far we lag behind the angels. How long have they been flying, traveling at the speed of light and remaining invisible? It makes us look like intellectual dwarfs.

Judge not,
that ye not be judged.

Matthew 7:1 KJV

Sometimes angels are people
simply willing to listen.

Angel on the Internet

She was young, living all alone, confused, and angry. She needed the money and had agreed to be a surrogate mother. But, now, with baby born and gone, she felt even more lonely and empty than ever.

Chatting on the internet was a diversion from reality. Most people ignored her when she started to type about her young, depressing life. But, tonight

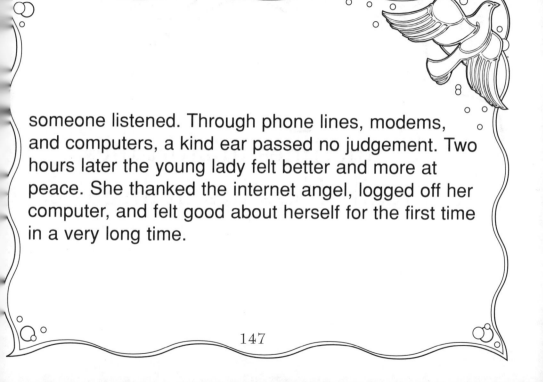

someone listened. Through phone lines, modems, and computers, a kind ear passed no judgement. Two hours later the young lady felt better and more at peace. She thanked the internet angel, logged off her computer, and felt good about herself for the first time in a very long time.

Sometimes misfortunes
are really blessings in disguise.

Angels are noble
guardians of God's glory.

And when we cried unto
the Lord, he heard our voice,
and sent an angel....

Numbers 20:16

Burnt Offering

All of a sudden smoke was escaping from the oven. The woman ran to rescue her wild blueberry pie which was on fire. Visions of the 19th century home insulated with sawdust igniting frightened her. She was so disappointed this had happened. As she sat outside, grieving over the charred pie, she heard cries from across the ocean bay, "Help, help, would somebody please help me?"

The woman looked over the cliff side to the water. She could not see anyone. Then, she looked down, only to discover her ten year old daughter wandering around disoriented and covered with blood, "Help, help, would somebody please help me?" Grabbing the little redhead, the father raced her to the van. The mother drove and prayed the entire 45 minute drive to the nearest hospital. On arrival, the injury had been cleaned, 5 rock shards were removed from between the girl's skull and skin, and nine stitches placed in her forehead. The girl would be okay.

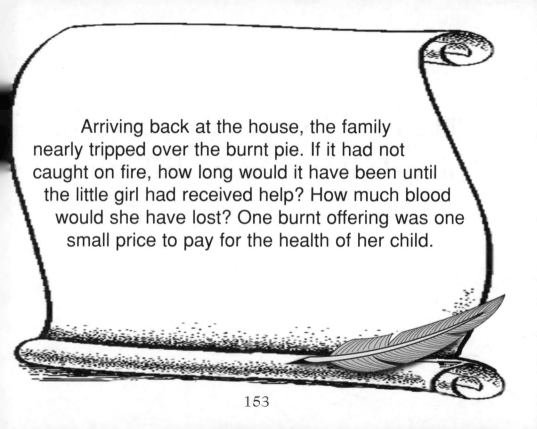

Arriving back at the house, the family nearly tripped over the burnt pie. If it had not caught on fire, how long would it have been until the little girl had received help? How much blood would she have lost? One burnt offering was one small price to pay for the health of her child.

It's hard to hear the voices of angels if you aren't listening.

In order to see angels,
it's more important to open
your heart than your eyes.

Sometimes it is necessary to nestle in the wings of an angel.

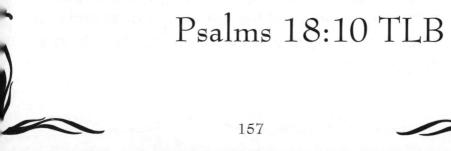

"Mounted on a mighty angel,
he sped swiftly to my aid
with the wings of wind."

Psalms 18:10 TLB

Sometimes Angels Travel by Plane

For the passengers on this single engine plane, it was the longest twenty minutes of their lives. Not far into this trip, warning lights flashed on the control panel and the pilot decided to turn around and head back to the airport, but he and his passengers would never make it there that day. The engine sputtered and quit. Gliding towards the earth, the pilot rehearsed the landscape over and over in his head. His only chance would be to try to land in a nearby swampy bog.

Meanwhile, the small group of passengers cried and prayed. Many thought about their families and loved ones. A mother wondered if she had spent enough time with her children while a man took out his brief case and started writing a very emotional final good bye letter to his wife. It was over, and every passenger on that plane had twenty minutes to think about it.

Coming out from some cloud cover, the pilot thought he had about 2000 feet until impact, only to realized that he had 200 feet. The thrust of the collision and the sound of the crash burned itself permanently into the minds of all the passengers.

Somehow, they all survived
and crawled out of the plane. The pilot was
still trapped inside, blood pouring from his head. When
the threat of explosion had passed, the passengers
rescued the very brave man to await help in the icy,
wet, cold bog.

A year later, during a television interview, the man
who wrote what he thought was his final letter to his
wife reported emphatically, "There were angels on that
plane that day. There were angels on that plane."

For with God
nothing shall be impossible.

Luke 2:37 KJB

Would you be comfortable having your angel write a biography on your life?

I think guardian angels spend most of their time guarding us from ourselves.

Strangers knock
on your door,
angels knock
on your heart.

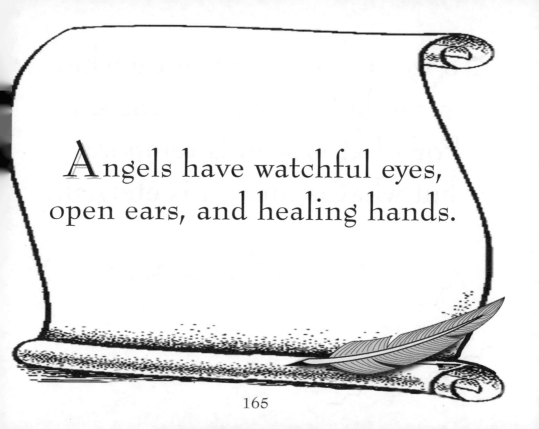

Angels have watchful eyes, open ears, and healing hands.

So we fix our eyes not on what is seen, but on what is unseen. For what is seen is temporary, but what is unseen is eternal.

2 Corinthians 4:18 NIV

...He will send his angel
on ahead of you...

Genesis 24:7 TLB

Other Titles by Great Quotations

301 Ways to Stay Young At Heart
The ABC's of Parenting
African-American Wisdom
Angel-grams
As A Cat Thinketh
Astrology for Cats
Astrology for Dogs
The Be-Attitudes
The Birthday Astrologer
Can We Talk
Celebrating Women
Chicken Soup
Chocoholic Reasonettes
The Cornerstones of Success
Daddy & Me
Erasing My Sanity
Fantastic Father, Dependable Dad
Golden Years, Golden Words
Graduation Is Just The Beginning
Grandma, I Love You
Happiness is Found Along The Way
High Anxieties
Hooked on Golf

I Didn't Do It
I'm Not Over the Hill
Ignorance is Bliss
Inspirations
Interior Design for Idiots
The Lemonade Handbook
Let's Talk Decorating
Life's Lessons
Life's Simple Pleasures
A Lifetime of Love
A Light Heart Lives Long
Looking for Mr. Right
Midwest Wisdom
Mommy & Me
Mother, I Love You
The Mother Load
Motivating Quotes
    for Motivated People
Mrs. Murphy's Laws
Mrs. Webster's Dictionary
My Daughter, My Special Friend
Only a Sister
The Other Species

Parenting 101
Pink Power
Reflections
Romantic Rhapsody
The Secret Language of Men
The Secret Language of Women
The Secrets in Your Face
The Secrets in Your Name
A Servant's Heart
Social Disgraces
Some Things Never Change
The Sports Page
Sports Widow
Stress or Sanity
A Teacher is Better Than
    Two Books
TeenAge of Insanity
Thanks from the Heart
Things You'll Learn...
A Touch of Friendship
Wedding Wonders
Words From The Coach
Working Woman's World

Great Quotations, Publishing Company
1967 Quincy Court
Glendale Heights, IL 60139 USA
Phone: 630-582-2800   Fax: 630-582-2813
http://www.greatquotations.com